MICHAEL ROSEN'S
BOOK
OF

NONSENSE

MICHAEL ROSEN'S BOOK OF NONSENSE

ILLUSTRATED BY CLARE MACKIE

MACDONALD YOUNG BOOKS

DEDICATIONS

FOR 6/455 HOLLOWAY ROAD AND ALL WHO SAILED IN HER

MICHAEL ROSEN

FOR SOLANNE, CAMILLE, FRED, NATASHA, INDIA, ISAMU, FRED, NED, KATIE,
NINA AND LACHIE.

CLARE MACKIE

First published in Great Britain in 1997 by
Macdonald Young Books, an imprint of
Wayland Books Ltd
61 Western Road
Hove
East Sussex BN3 1JD

Find Wayland on the internet at http://www.wayland.co.uk

Poems © Michael Rosen
Illustrations © Clare Mackie

Edited by Wendy Knowles
Designed by David Fordham

Printed and bound in Portugal by Edições ASA
Typeset by MATS, Southend-on-Sea, Essex

ISBN   07500 2192 6

DIS CONTENTS

INTRODUCTION

This is not the end of the book. It's the beginning. And while
I think of it, this is not a potato, it's a book. Because it's a
book it's not full of sandwiches, it's full of words and
pictures. This is the end of my introduction.

Michael Rosen.

Aren't you glad it was so interesting and useful?...

Are you wearing jeans?   No, I'm wearing mine.

I'm on T.V.

It could be a
swimming pool,
couldn't it?

SPLISH

When I walk across the room
I hear a splash and a splish.
There's something under the rug.
I think it's a jellyfish.

splash

7

ROSIE ROSIE

........no cake left for us again.

The dog told the cat
the cat told the queen
Rosie Rosie's birthday cake's
stuck in the washing machine.

It sploshed it
it washed it
and Dad had a fit.

Rosie Rosie's whipped it out
and eaten every bit.

......well at least
the cake was clean.

REALLY?

He had a little sticker
and he had a little ticket
and he took the little sticker
and he stuck it to the ticket.

Now he hasn't got a sticker
and he hasn't got a ticket.
He's got a bit of both
which he calls a little sticket.

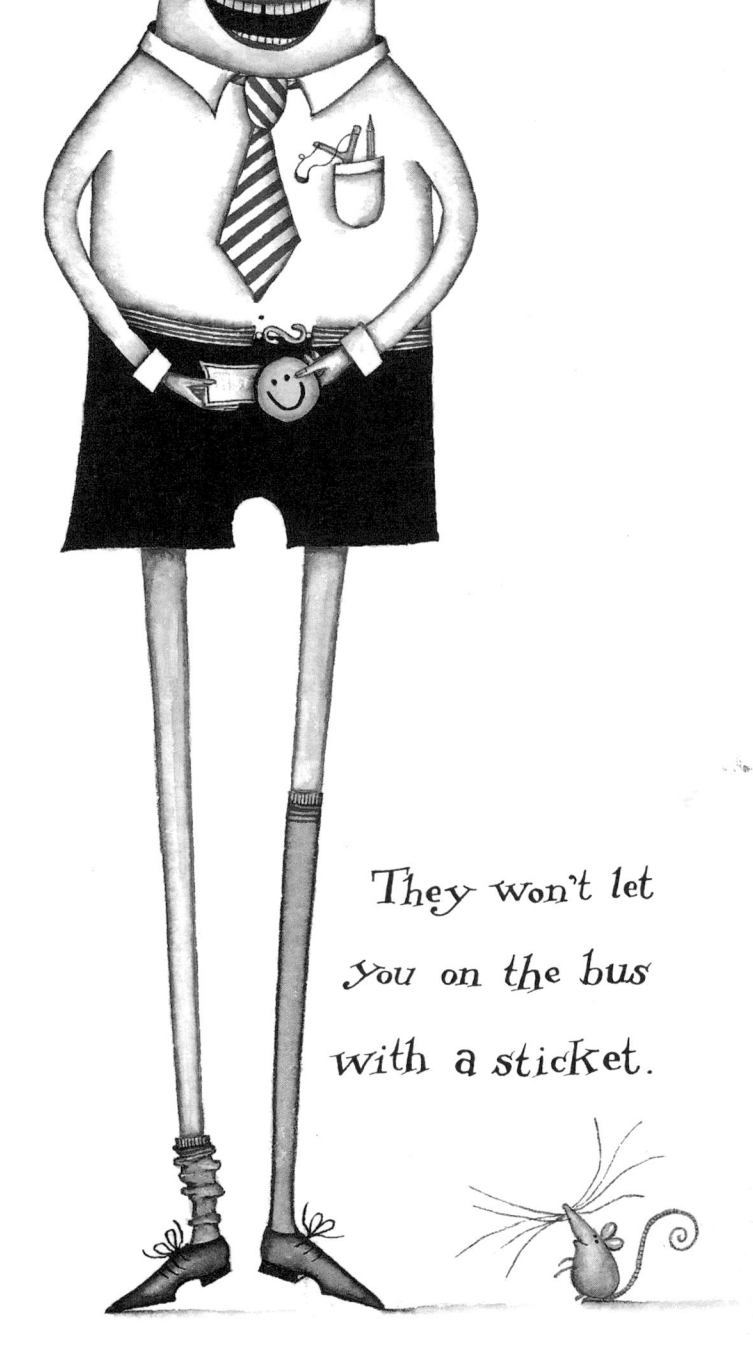

They won't let
you on the bus
with a sticket.

HELP

Help, help
nothing's right
I can't find my ears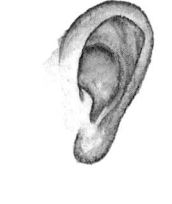
and my pants are too tight.

There's a clock in my sock
there's a rose up my nose
there's an egg on my leg
and there's a stink in the sink.

Help, help
I've had enough
I can't find my eyes
and the going's getting tough.

There's bread in my bed
there's flies in my fries
there's a slug in the jug
and there's a ghost on my toast.

Help, help
I'm in a mess.
Have you got my head?
The cat says yes.

The cat says yes,
the donkey says **No.**
The hamster in the swimming pool
says he doesn't know.

... search me ...

WHEN DINOSAURS FOOLED THE EARTH.

VERY-LOUD-ASAURUS

Seen at big concerts and in school yards.

AREN'T-YOU-GLAD-YOU-SAURUS?

No.

SHUT-THE-DAURUS

Have you seen my dinosaur?

FLAT-ON-THE-FLAURUS

I can see you.

You can't see me!

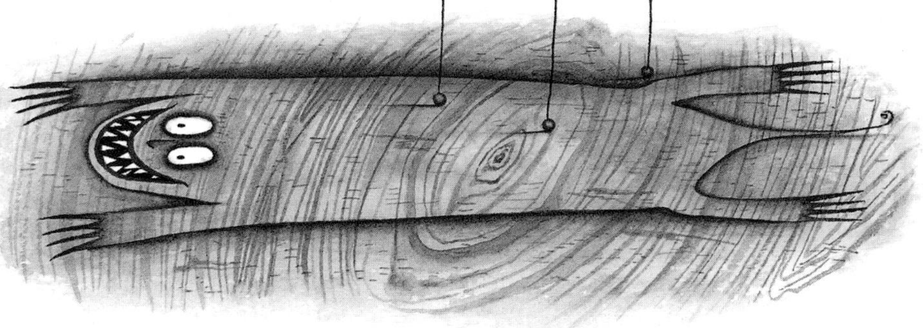

Can be used
in the bath as a sponge.

VERY-POROUS

Angel Delight.

HEAVENLY-CHORUS

MY-SIGN-IS-TAURUS

This month look out for a large dinosaur who answers to the name 'Rex'.

GLAD-I'M-NOT-A-WALRUS

I'm glad I'm not a GLAD-I'M-NOT-A-WALRUS.

ROAD

In the middle of the road it's lonely
the cars go whistling by
I've got no one to talk to
apart from a passing fly.

The noise from the traffic is awful.
My ears are going to burst.
I've been in some terrible places
but I know this is the worst.

I remember being up a chimney
the fire was blazing bright
I remember being in a forest
on a dark and stormy night.

But here the traffic is roaring
I can't describe the stink.
My eyes are weeping buckets
I can hardly hear myself think.

❖ T.V. CATS ❖

I'm all alone and lonely.
Stuck in the middle of the road.
I'm trying very hard to be brave
I'm a common or garden toad.

WRONG

It's all gone wrong
the singer's lost her song.
She lost the key to her apple
and the bell has lost its bong.

What should she do?
The pickle's in a stew
She lost the switch to her orange
and the shine has lost its shoe.

FRIDGE

There's nothing in the fridge.
There's nothing in the fridge.
Just two frozen peas
and Uncle Joe's sneeze.
There's nothing in the fridge
nothing in the fridge.

NOTE TO CHILDREN

Frozen peas are O.K.

but don't eat sneezes.

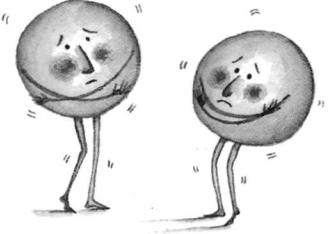

DIGGEDY-DO

Diggedy-do
Diggedy-do
The train is late
what shall we do?
Diggedy-do
Diggedy-do
The train is late
what a to-do.
Grandpa coughed
and the wheels fell off.
Diggedy-do
Diggedy-do.

What's the opposite of Diggedy-do?

Diggedy-don't!

BEANS

It's bad out there
it's scary, it's weird
you thought it was hard
but it's worse than you feared.

Next time they say it'll be 'cloudy'
do you know what that really means?
Yes, of course it's going to rain
but it's going to rain baked beans.

Millions and millions of beans
are going to fall out of the sky
all over me and you
I promise you this is no lie.

The streets will be covered with beans;
over houses and cars and vans.
Your hair will be sticky with beans
there'll be beans all over your hands.

Towers will drip with the juice.
Houses will all disappear.
It's going to be something that lasts
for anything up to a year.

Bulldozers will be called into action;
they'll try to move the muck,
but after just a few minutes
most of them will be stuck.

People will go out with hoses;
buckets, jugs and cups
and hundreds of hungry people
will try to gobble it up.

It'll take ten years in all
to clean up every little bean.
So remember – next time you hear the word 'cloudy'
you know what it will mean . . .

FOOTBALLS

There's something I think should be said.
And this is how it ought to be put:
A football shouldn't be round – *or oval*
It should look like it sounds – like a foot.

Should a basketball look like a basket?

THE
LONG AND
AMAZING
STORY OF
WHAT HAPPENED
WHEN WE WENT
TO THE GAME
LAST WEEK....

I was bored.
They scored.
We roared.

IF. . . .

If Dennis plays tennis
and Rocky plays hockey
and Rolf plays golf
and Tess plays chess
and Marty does karate
and Ludo does Judo
and Rose rows . . .

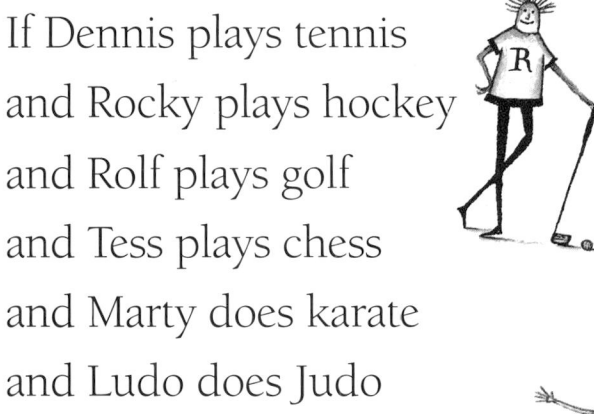

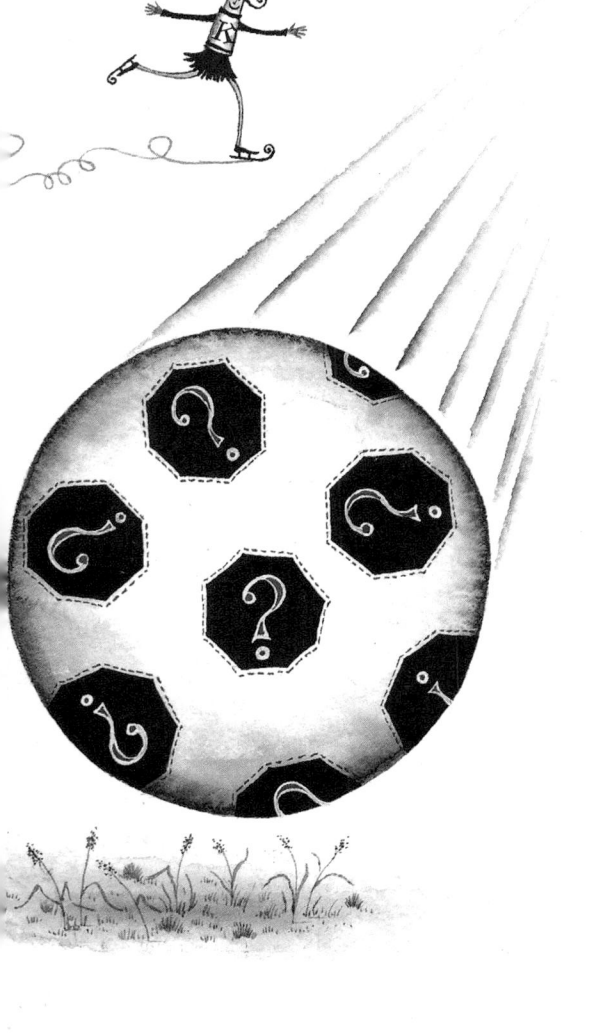

. . . and if Kim can swim
and Dee can ski
and Myrtle can hurdle
and Clint can sprint
and Kate can skate
and Mo can throw
and (like I said)
Rose rows . . .

. . . then who is there round here
who can play football?

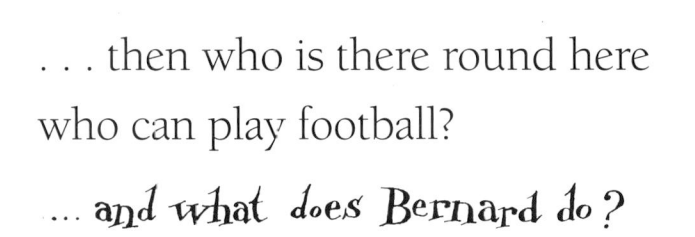

. . . and what does Bernard do?

FOOTLING AROUND

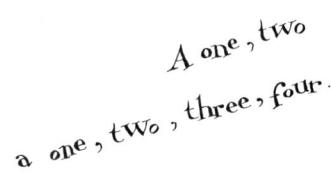
A one, two
a one, two, three, four...

. . . footle flop doodle
footle flop doodle.

You can flap your flapper
you can flop your flopper
you can clap your clapper
you can clop your clopper.

Footle flop doodle
footle flop doodle.

You can foot your footle
you can fit your fittle
you can dood your doodle
you can did your diddle.

Footle flop doodle
footle flop doodle.

6 LIMERICKS...

A young man with wobbly eyes
used to muddle his g's and his y's.
When he said 'guess'
I guess he meant 'yes'
and 'yugs' was how he said 'guys'.

A man with an enormous nose
used to put on fantastic shows.
In his nose he'd squeeze
a swarm of bees,
a cabbage and most of his toes.

This is disgusting and shouldn't be in this book.

There was a young man with a pimple
who said everything in life is simple.
For weeks and weeks
he sucked in his cheeks
and now his pimple's a dimple.

A boy who told tales called Peter
had news about a huge cheetah.
'What it was doing,'
he said, 'was chewing
a medium-sized thin crust pizza.'

There was an old man from Wales
who was always cutting his nails.
The bits could be found
in a pile on the ground
being eaten by giant snails.

boo!

GOOD MOO GUIDE

If he studied a dove he could learn how to coo.

FROM BOO TO MOO
DR MOO
5 GUYS NAMED MOO
HOW TO SAY MOO

moo-oo!

There was an old man from Crewe
who wanted to know how to moo.
He studied a cow
to try and learn how
but all he could do was boo.

BILLY'S BULLY BOYS

The people upstairs
are making a horrible noise.
We know who it is:
it's Billy's Bully Boys.

They come in late.
They've got hairy legs.
They keep pet slugs,
and put custard on their eggs.

They wear dirty jackets.
They don't bother with shirts.
On Sunday afternoons
they wear yellow skirts.

Mr Billy's Bully Boys
like to spit and cough.
I know what I'd like:
I wish they'd clear off.

❖ T.V. ❖ CATS ❖

THE NEWS

Here is The News:
'Two incredible shoes.
Two incredible shoes.
That's The News.

When it rains
they walk down drains.

They glow
in the snow.

They grizzle
in a drizzle.

They sneeze
in a breeze.

They get warm
in a storm.

• T.V. • CATS •

HELP!

THANK YOU

They go soggy
when it's foggy.

They've even hissed
in a mist.

But
(sad to say)
there came a terrible frost.
This is what happened:
they got lost.'

That was The News.
Two incredible shoes.
Two incredible shoes.
That was The News.

We're on The News tonight.

31

BLEEP

cheep CHEEP

Wait for the bleep
wait for the bleep
bleeps on the phone
bleep bleep bleep.

Wait for the bleep
wait for the bleep
bleeps on machines
bleeps in my sleep.

bleep

Bleep on the freezer
bleep on the monitor
bleep on the crossing lights
bleep on the computer.

Bleep

Bleep

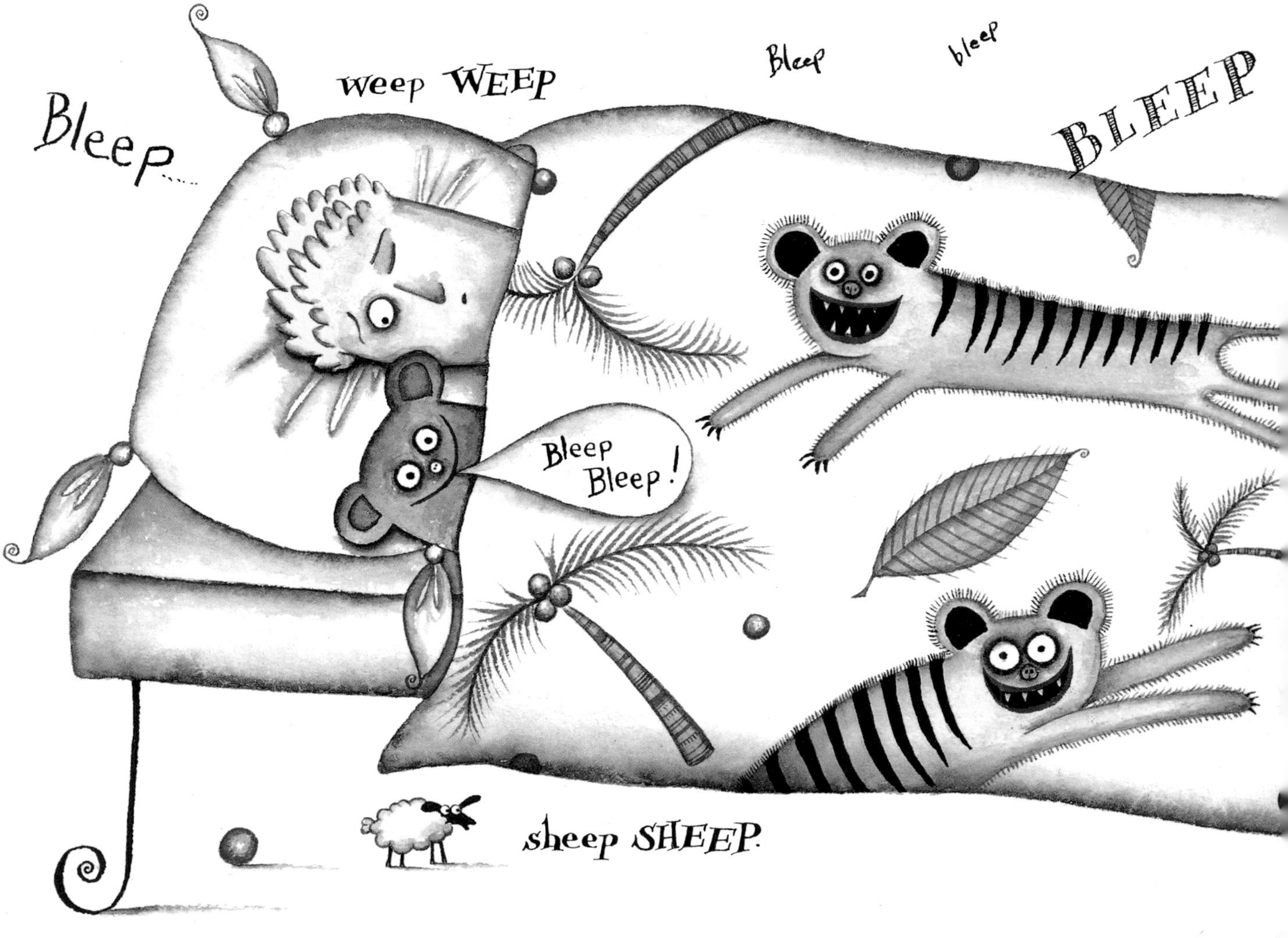

Bleep.

weep WEEP

Bleep

bleep

BLEEP

Bleep Bleep!

sheep SHEEP.

GET UP

Get up Joe
Get up Eddie
the tea's in the teapot
the sausages are ready.

Get up Eddie
Get up Joe.
Eddie says yes
Joe says no.

So, cover him up with cornflakes,
pour milk on his head,
put sugar in his ears
and leave him in his bed.

THE DOG

Floppy old Poppy
and Whiskers Jim
looked for the dog
and couldn't find him.
He was away
on a trip to the stars,
eating butter
in a house on Mars.

Why doesn't he have
bread with his butter?

34

POLYPROPYLENE

I know someone
called Polly Wolly Doodle.

I'm a mat on the floor
just by the door.
I'm tough, I'm mean
I'm polypropylene.

Poly, poly,
poly, prop

prop, prop
propylene

propylene
keeps it clean
poly, poly
propylene.

WELCOME

I'm a mat and I matter.

GO TO BED

Go to bed Lizzie,
Go to bed Jane,
It's far too late,
Don't be a pain.

Jane's under the table,
Lizzie's eating peas.
Mum's in the bath,
Dad's going to sneeze.

Go to bed Jane,
Go to bed Lizzie,
Jane's dozing off
but Lizzie's too busy.

DO YOU KNOW WHAT?

Do you know what?
said Tiny Tony,
I've found my foot
and it feels all bony.

Do you know what?
said Auntie Flo,
I think this lump
is a bone in my toe.

Do you know what?
said Mrs Jones
but I think our feet
are full of bones.

Tony, Flo and Mrs Jones
are absolutely right.
There are bones
in our feet.

BIPS

Look out,
look out
the Bips are out.

They leer,
they sneer,
they put on nasty grins.
They fight,
they bite,
they lick their sweaty chins.

They mutter,
they splutter,
they show their greasy
fangs.
They grunt,
they hunt,
they go about in gangs.

They yell,
they smell,
they wave their little flags.
And they keep
dead sheep
in dirty little bags.

Look out,
look out
the Bips are out.
Look out,
look out
the Bips are out.

MARY ANNE

Little Mary, Mary Anne
was really quite fantastic.
She wasn't like her friends:
'cos she was made of elastic.

She'd roll herself up
to become very small,
then jump up and down
and bounce like a ball.

She'd tie her leg to the gate
and make her other leg hop,
the elastic would stretch
and take her to the shop.

She could leave a room
and you wouldn't mind
but then you'd discover
she'd left her eyes behind.

40

What happens if you're made of old sausages?

She might be upstairs
eating jelly;
while you're downstairs
she'd tickle your belly.

She could tie her hand to the table
(this was a wicked trick)
stretch out and let go
and give you a terrible flick.

One day a man came
to measure Mary Anne
from foot to head
and from hand to hand.

With no further ado
the girl was fetched
and with a smile on her face
she stretched and stretched.

She stretched and stretched
this amazing girl
she stretched and stretched
right round the world.

This made her so hot
she began to smoke.
There was a sudden snap
and she suddenly broke.

It was a terrible shame
that it was all so drastic
but that's what happens
if you're made of elastic.

MORE, MORE, MORE

supermarket shopping
I can't stop stopping
I can't walk by
I buy, buy, buy
everything on the shelf
I want for myself
everything I see
I want for me, me, me
I'm gonna load up a sack
you can't hold me back

I want more, more, more
more, more, more
more's not enough
give me more stuff
crunch, crunch, crunch
munch, munch, munch

THE BUS

I woke up this morning,
went for a ride on the bus.
A donkey got on
and made a terrible fuss.

She wanted some straw
laid out on her seat.
She wanted some grass
laid under her feet.

The driver said no,
and drove off quick.
The donkey didn't like it
and gave him a kick.

If this donkey tries
to get on your bus
call the police.

TAG-ALONG

Little Johnny Tag-along
wants a pat on the head.
He does as he's told
and gets a kick instead.

WHO AM I?

My face fell off my head
and landed on the floor,
wriggled about awhile
then galloped out the door.

It scared a cat in the yard.
It ate some bread and jam.
It fell into a puddle –
now I don't know who I am.

You ought to face up to this problem.

YUM-YUM

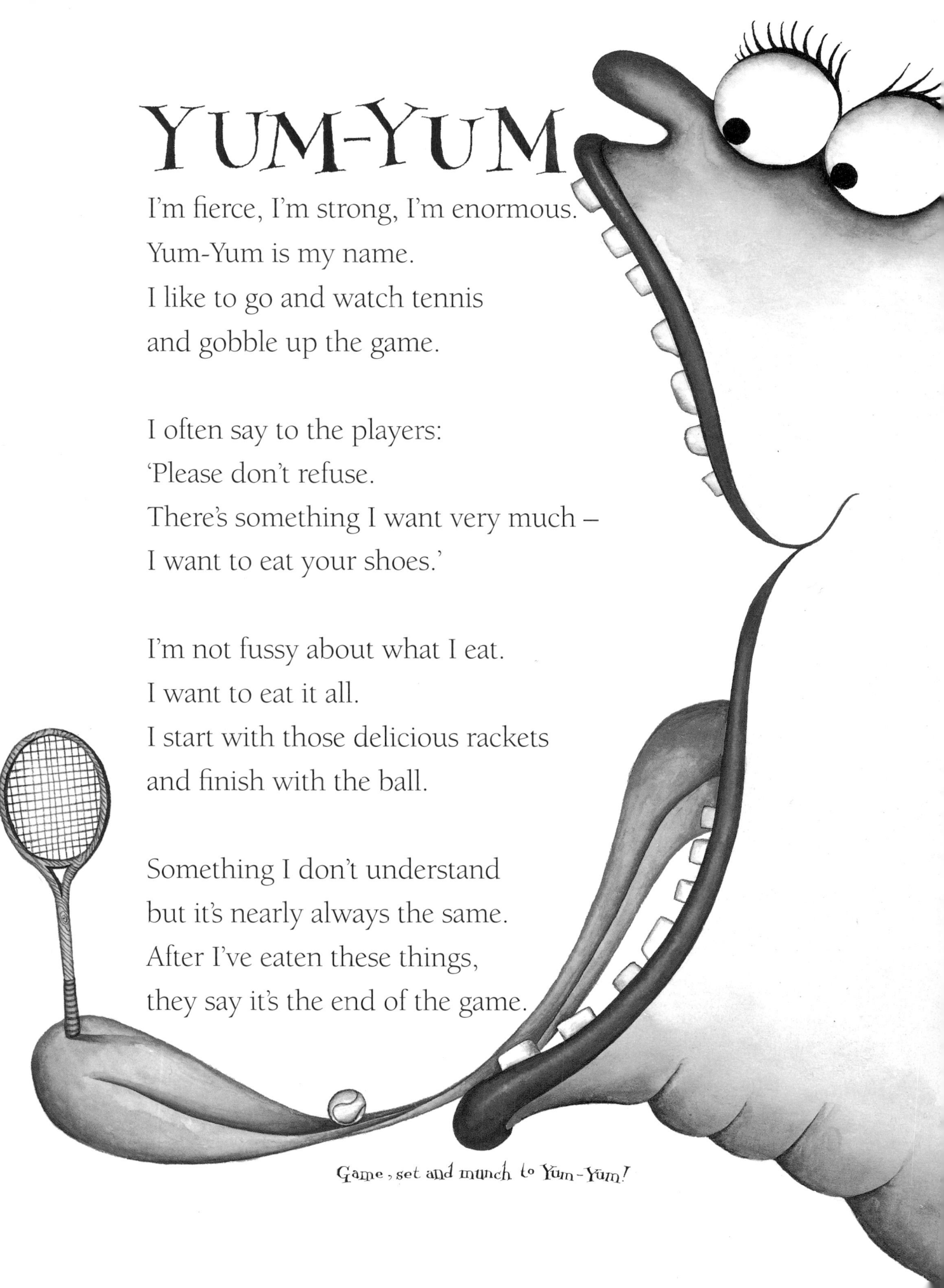

I'm fierce, I'm strong, I'm enormous.
Yum-Yum is my name.
I like to go and watch tennis
and gobble up the game.

I often say to the players:
'Please don't refuse.
There's something I want very much –
I want to eat your shoes.'

I'm not fussy about what I eat.
I want to eat it all.
I start with those delicious rackets
and finish with the ball.

Something I don't understand
but it's nearly always the same.
After I've eaten these things,
they say it's the end of the game.

Game, set and munch to Yum-Yum!

❧ T.V. ❧ CATS ❧

YESTERDAY

Isn't this the name of a song?

The day before yesterday
I think I'll go to school.
I think I'll take a walk
in the local swimming pool.

The T.V.'s broken
so I think I'll watch The News.
I'll be going out barefoot
in my sister's shoes.

I don't like her,
so I call her my friend.
When I leave
I'll start at the end.

the End (start here)

...and a cat can bat...

POSTSCRIPT

This is not the beginning of the book. It's the end.
Actually it's not quite the end. But that's it for now ...
(for the time being)

not quite THE END